Ignorance
Is
Contagious!

Ignorance Is Contagious!

Stories by:
Abdul Majid

TRUE STORIES AND LIFE LESSONS OF
OOLISHNESS, STUPIDITY, AND BUFFOONERY

Life Lessons by:
James LeGrand
Author of "Evolve!"

iUniverse, Inc.
Bloomington

Ignorance Is Contagious!
True stories and Life Lessons of Foolishness, Stupidity, and Buffoonery

iUniverse books may be ordered through booksellers or by contacting:

iUniverse
1663 Liberty Drive
Bloomington, IN 47403
www.iuniverse.com
1-800-Authors (1-800-288-4677)

ISBN: 978-1-4759-4602-4 (sc)
ISBN: 978-1-4759-4603-1 (ebk)

Printed in the United States of America

iUniverse rev. date: 09/21/2012

Ig.no.rant

Pronunciation: (ig-ner-uh nt)

Function: adjective

Definition: 1. (Caribbean) a quarrelsome and aggressive attitude

2. Lacking in knowledge or training; unlearned

Con.ta.gion

Pronunciation: (kuh n-tey-juh n)

Function: noun

Definition: (Literary) the spreading of an attitude or emotion from person to person among a number of people

Dedications

Abdul Majid

In memory of Elena Foster Majid
August 15, 1950 to March 17, 2002

I heard a person once say "All I ever wanted was the opportunity to have an opportunity". If I had the opportunity, I would love to thank you in person for every kind word you said, every hug I received and every smile you gave me, because in the end that is all I can remember. Unfortunately, wishing is for children and all I have are those fond memories of those yester years that once were. My only regret is that I wish I could have done more with the little time we had. I hope that with whatever time I have left on this planet, I can make you proud of the man you raised. I will see you again.

Love Always, Abdul Majid

James LeGrand

To find your soul mate is a rare gift that I will forever appreciate. I am thankful for my soul mate, Christina LeGrand and our three beautiful children—D'ante, Jordan and Isabella.

I wish everyone could experience the happiness that has become my norm every single day.

Contents

Introduction

"Everything in life is either a lesson or a blessing but it's your job to figure out which is which because sometimes what you think is a lesson is actually a blessing and what you think is a blessing is actually a lesson." From Ahmed Majid, my father, my mentor, the person I'd most like to be like when I get older and all around good guy.

In March of 2012 I was asked to speak at an event called "Man Up Mondays" in Newark, New Jersey. Pastor Tyanna Motley organized the event. It was designed for the older generation of men to talk to the younger generation to impart some wisdom to them about some of the obstacles they will encounter in their lifetime. In doing my research leading up to this event, I discovered that as of the November 2009 U.S Census Bureau, there are 13.7 million parents in the United States and out of that number 84% of them are from single mother household.

Now as a man who had a father and several brothers growing up I know the importance of having an older male figure to help you navigate around all of the potholes life has to offer. So me being me, I got excited about the opportunity to help some young confused kid who was probably like me in my adolescence. So I armed myself with every statistic I could find, readying myself to fight all of the misleading information, untruths and overall ignorant shit we tell each other at that age . . . but here's the rub.

I think I may have been the 3rd of 4th speaker at this event and as I watched the preceding speaker do the exact thing I was ready do I started to get really nervous. I wasn't nervous because of having to give a speech, I started to get nervous from the reaction I saw the kids give the speeches before mine. These kids were by no stretch of the imagination rowdy or belligerent. They were so bored . . . . and bored kids don't process information well, but what they will do is fidget or fall asleep (I swear one kid was in full REM sleep . . . and I mean that good sleep, the kind where you drool with your mouth open . . . that sleep).

So now quick, fast and in a hurry, I had to change my approach to this whole thing. The thing I wasn't going to do was take an L (loss) like the guy in front of me who was going down faster than groupies at the NBA Draft. I started to think back to all of the great information I retained and how that information was delivered. It seemed to me that all of the important life lessons I remembered were told through humorous stories accompanied by the lesson they learned from it. So that's exactly what I did. I went up there and told several stories about things I've seen and things that happened to me. As sure as I am black, these kids started to get involved and to participate in the discussion.

Well, this book is an extension of that event. What I wish to accomplish is to impart on you the life lessons I've learned by ingeminating some humorous but true accounts of things that have happened to me or have been witness to with the life lessons I've learned from them with the help of my brother James LeGrand, Life Strategist and author of "Evolve!: Live Spiritually Every Day, Every Where, and in Every Way".

My attempt was to entertain you as well as educate you through my foolish misadventures. I hope that you get a good laugh from this book. Most importantly, I hope you are informed by the lessons learned. If it helps you avoid some of the obstacles that I went through, then going through them was well worth it.

Warning!

The stories you are about to read are 100% true. Names have been changed to protect the ignorant, the guilty and the stupid.

If you wish to maintain your self-respect, sense of intelligence, and reputation, please, do not try these events at home!!

Parental discretion is advised!

Take 1: The Wing Man

The Story, by Abdul Majid

In February of 2004 during New York's fashion week, a friend of mine (who will remain nameless) calls me up and asks me to do him a favor. He said he's been talking to this woman who is a model for a couple of weeks, but she won't go out with him unless she can bring her cousin. He wanted to use my "man pretty" visage to keep her cousin occupied while he tries his full court press on the model. Now, I normally don't do things like this because the role of the wingman is a thankless job that never seems to play out the way you've envisioned it in your mind. It's tantamount to being cannon fodder for every war a black man has participated in that preceded segregation, and I ain't about to be Crispus Attucks (and if you don't know who he is you should be ashamed of yourself . . . but that's exactly my point).

Trepidatiously I agreed to the date for two of the following reasons: 1. I'm thinking if she's a model, video ass shaker or otherwise, then her cousin must be off the meat rack (and by meat rack I mean an abundance of ass and titties . . . you usually take an L on the face . . . BBD said "You can't trust a big butt and a smile," but big titties have always been pretty trustworthy in my book).

2. My (so called) boy is gassing me up on some high octane shit about how fine she is. So poof pow, two days later we go to Harlem to hang out in the models apartment where I get to meet her zaftig, if not buxom, cousin for the first time.

We get to the apartment, and as I'm reciting to myself "Big money no whammies", over and over, my boy knocks on the door and I hear a pleasant voice that says "Coming." The door swings open and there stands the cousin. This (alleged) woman stood around 5'10, looked like Akon and was built like Karl Malone (yes nigga the Mailman). So right about now I'm fucking Yosemite Sam upset! My first impulse was to get on my Harriet Tubman shit and run for my freedom, but I've watched one too many "When animals attack" videos so I know what a wild bear can do to fleeing prey . . . so I just stood there trying to make no sudden movements.

So instead of me deserting his ass like a slave fighting for the Confederacy (and against his personal interest), me being the good wing man that I am, I go along with this human sacrifice and walk myself into this Mel Gibson, Apocalypto ritual chamber of death. The evening goes off with out a hitch . . . or as well as a Death Row Records audition can go as you wait for the inevitable beat down. Towards the end of the night, everybody's drinking alcohol (except me), feeling comfortable (except me), so we start to play a game of spades . . .

. . . . but before I finish this story, here is a quick PSA . . . Never do anything on a first introduction that you wouldn't normally do in any regular circumstance. I haven't had coffee in years, but that night I was so tired from the let down that I tried one of those espresso shots and maaaaan I was wired . . . but then 30 minutes later I crashed and was more tired than before I drank the damn thing. So by the end of the night, I wound up drinking four more of those things just to stay even and I got all twitchy, sweaty and whatnot. I looked like a straight heroin (pronounced hair-ron) addict . . . and then came the shits . . . and that motherfucka was violent . . . I'm talking roid rage violent . . . I'm talking Suge Knight violent . . . it felt like my ass was holding Vanilla Ice over a balcony by his ankles . . . and then it killed Biggie. So routine is of the utmost importance when doing anything for the 1st time . . . and now back to the story already in progress . . .

Now, already irritated by the nights events (and gastric trauma), during the game of spades the cousin, who for the sake of the story we'll call "Deebo," reneged on a hand. I immediately call her on it and an argument ensues.

Me
Yo, you just reneged

Deebo
(With an attitude)
No I didn't

Me
Yes you did. You cut my diamond two hands ago and you just threw out a diamond.

Deebo
No I didn't. You just mad cuz you loosing.

Me
Nigga check your books

Deebo
I ain't checkin' shit.

Me
Then I ain't playing

Deebo
Look I'm tired of "argering" so I'ma be "Pacific" when I say this . . . . it's just a game so if we playing lets play.

Me
(Confused)
You gonna be Pacific? Like the ocean nigga?

Deebo
(With an attitude)
That's what I said!

Me
You win.

Ignorance is contagious people . . . . learn when to say when.

You can't pick your family but you can pick your friends so choose wisely.

The Life Lesson, by James LeGrand

True friends are willing to do almost anything for one another as long as there is honesty and trust between them. Betray that trust, and you might lose a friend.

In this situation, one friend was not fully honest with the other on what to expect in this dating experience. When expectations don't match the reality, discomfort is often the result. One friend selfishly gets what they want in the situation (the ability to date the model) while the other friend is left feeling lied to, taken advantage of, and unwilling to trust that friend in the future.

Dates come and go, but true friendships are rare and difficult to come by. If we are willing to sabotage our truest friendships over the temporary pleasure a date might bring, then what else are we willing to sacrifice our friendships for? In the end, is it really worth losing a true friend's trust over something so fleeting?

The lesson here is that when you have a friend that is willing to support you and your ambitions, you owe it to them to give them the facts in an honest and straight-forward way. Without that level of straight-forward communication, you won't have that friend available as your wing man (or wing woman) in the future.

Take 2: You Just Talkin' Cuz You Got Lips

The Story, by Abdul Majid

In October of 2008 I went out on a date with this lovely woman. We just came from seeing a movie at the Loews Theater on 34th Street between 8th and 9th in Manhattan. We're both a little hungry, so we decide to go to the Dallas BBQ's on 23 and 8th (Dallas BBQ's; yeah I know but whatever). We get to the restaurant and the hostess sits us in the back of the restaurant in one of those two person tables next to another black couple.

Now I'm not one to be nosey, but I look over at the table next to us to acknowledge the couple sitting next to us being that they were so close . . . by the way . . . to anyone who owns, manages or works at a Dallas BBQ's, if you're gonna give people that much food and alcohol (and I'm not complaining about that), it would be wise to sit people a little further apart because niggaitis (or "the itis" for my non black friends) will turn a pleasant meal into a dinner with the Klumps (Hercules, Hercules!!!).

So like I was say saying, I look over towards the table directly next to us and I see a really thin man, neatly dressed with a slightly nerdy look to him. The woman was fat as all outside with a gangsta ass blond weave and a shiny Puff Daddy "Mo Money, Mo Problems" sweat suit on (take dat, take dat, take dat). Now I could tell from the rip that they were toasted, because you could smell the alcohol from a distance and they look a little two sheets to the wind to begin with. So they get the bill and like most men will do, he picks up the bill and looks at it. The woman sits there and continues to eat (cuz most women don't like to come out the pocket . . . but that's a another lesson for another day.) All of a sudden, he gets an annoyed look on his face and he says out loud.

The Man
How the fuck the bill get this god damn high?

The Woman
I don't know nigga we was eatin'

The Man
Nah nigga, YOU was eatin'. All I had was some chicken wings and a margarita.

The Woman
Na ah, don't even act like I ate all this food by myself.

The Man
Everybody in this room knows you ate all that food by yourself.

The Woman
See nigga you ain't shit

The Man
Fuck you bitch, the first time I met you I knew
you wasn't shit . . . . I just wanted the pussy.

The Woman
And the 1st time you dropped your pants it
looked like your balls were hitchhiking cuz you
was all thumbs.

AT THAT POINT I LOST IT!!!

Your problems aren't for the whole world to know.

The Life Lesson, by James LeGrand

Nobody wins during a public confrontation over a private issue, as it almost always leads to public humiliation.

Whether you are married, dating or just out with friends, it's important to not discuss potentially embarrassing topics in public. In this true story, the "gentleman" wasn't questioning the restaurant about the bill. He clearly knew that the bill was correct. What he was doing was insulting his date. In like fashion, she felt insulted and retaliated with a much more personal insult.

A more appropriate response by the man in this relationship would have been to wait until they were in private to discuss the matter if he felt she over indulged. Another avenue might have been to pay the check since the charges were already acquired, and to be better prepared financially for their next outing. A third option would have been to slow down on the alcohol consumption to ensure he didn't say anything he would regret later.

The next time you have a private issue in a public setting, be sure to take the conversation to a private setting to discuss it. Anything less than that will almost guarantee embarrassment for you and the one you are with.

Take 3: W . . . T . . . F!?!?

The Story, by Abdul Majid

As an adult, have you ever been speaking to your family and hear some shit that you really, really didn't want to hear? I just got off the phone with my cousin who is one of my mother's cousins from Panama. She's more like my aunt then a cousin for two reasons: 1. She's older and you're supposed to giver her that respect. 2. Her and my mother grew up together after her father died (long story that I'll tell you about some other time). She lived with her family, so they're more like sisters than cousins.

I've known this woman all my life, but we've gotten extremely close since my mother past away in 2002. Now, here's how our conversation went . . . . mind you, she's from Brooklyn and has a slight Spanish/Caribbean accent so everything said has a slightly more comedic element to it.

Me
A, what's up

Her
I was wondering if you could come by tomorrow and take me to Costco.

Me

Okay what time?

Her
Maybe around 1 or 1:30. Everybody's coming by around 5:30 / 6, and I need some stuff cuz mi gon make a mean cook up.

Me
Alright sounds good

Her
I remember my ex husband use to love my food you know . . . . too bad he ain't shit.

Me
Ah well you're better off with out him

Her
(After several seconds of silence)
Yeah but that man sure could sling a cock . . . . ooooh child let me tell you!!!

I'M LIKE WHAT THE FUCK !!! All that extra shit at the end wasn't even necessary . . . . but I didn't say that . . . just sat there in an awkward silence . . . I mean what do you say after someone throws cock slinging into the conversation . . ."Really? Do tell" . . . Nah son . . . nah!

Grown folks business ain't for the little people.

The Life Lesson, by James LeGrand

We must all respect the disconnect that exists between older and younger generations.

Before engaging in a conversation that can be interpreted as offensive or edgy, remember who your audience is. If there is a chance that your comment may offend them, think a little longer before you speak.

In this instance, a respected elder figure launched into what could only be called "TMI" (too much information) with a person from a younger generation that was surprised by the comment. Similarly, there are many people from younger generations that speak to their parents, grand parents and other elder figures in ways that disrespect their age, generation, and position in the family or society.

To avoid uncomfortable situations, keep in mind whom you are talking to, where you are, and what you are saying.

Take 4: Yes We Can . . . Obama '09

The Story, by Abdul Majid

I come from a family of very intellectually curious people. We may not have all lived up to our fullest potential, but there still exists a level of curiosity whether it be politically, socially or religiously. Well, during one of the more depressed chapters of my life in 2008, I took a trip to Florida to stay with my dad for a couple of months so I could try to get my life back in order.

See, after the attacks on September 11, 2001 my life began to take a downward spiral. Not that anything directly happed to me or my family from the events, but everything around me took a turn for the worst. In December of the same year, I was laid off from a job I loved. Then in March of 2002 my mother died and several months after that, my younger brother went to jail . . . . and then it really got bad.

Not being able to find a steady job at the previous financial level, I was just getting by on working freelance gigs and running through all of my saving. Things didn't look up for quite some time . . . and I'm talking years!!! So, 6 years rolls by and I'm down in Florida with my father and stepmother for 3 months still depressed, trying to get back to where it was before or at least to be able to sustain myself.

Now they say the thing about depression is that it makes you want to sleep all day and it keeps you up at night, and my depression wasn't any different. I do have to say that even through all of my whiny bullshit, my vanity still got the better of me and I still maintain a decent grooming habit and hygiene regimen. So one day I drove to the 24 hour Walmart at like 3 am to get some Tide because I needed to wash clothes. For some reason I started this habit of working out and doing all of my everyday chores at night because I guess it was less embarrassing or so it seemed to me (they say pride comes before the fall).

So I get the laundry detergent and I'm standing fifth in line behind an old white woman, an Indian man and two thuggish looking black men. Now even at my worst, intellectual curiosity is still there . . . dormant, but still there. So it wasn't out of the ordinary for me to listen in on the two thuggish looking black men's conversation, when they start talking about the Iraq war and Barack Obama.

Thug 1
If he gets elected I heard that nigga Barack is gonna be letting motherfuckas come home.

Thug 2
Yeah my mans and them is over there right now.

Thug 1
So now that they're coming home, you think they ever gonna get Bin Ladin?

Thug 2
I don't know but I'm not worried about him cuz it's that other mutherfucka we gots to get.

Thug 1
Who the fuck you talkin' bout son?

Thug 2
You know that motherfucka Muqtada al Sadr!

Thug 1
Who the fuck is Muqtada al Sadr?

Thug 2
You know over in Iraq and shit . . . . that nigga's the Insurgent General!!!

INSURGENT GENERAL!!!

I LAUGHED MY MOTHERFUCKING ASS OFF!!! And if you can still find something to laugh about then your life is fucked up, then it really isn't that bad off.

The key word in "Yes We Can" is We.

The Life Lesson, by James LeGrand

Now more than ever, we must all engage in political activism.

Most people are engaged in the political process by just repeating the same sound bites they hear from their favorite news provider without any additional thought or research. Even then, people often misquote what they've heard, as this story humorously demonstrates. Its time to stop regurgitating and to start putting serious thought into your own opinions and what you can do to get involved in the process.

There are consequences to politics. The areas of war, debt, finances, real estate and personal freedom are just a few of the areas that have held a recurring role in our most dominate news cycles over the past 10 years. Complaining to those that can't engage in serious change does nothing but blow off steam. Unless you are directly involved in some capacity, your voice is simply not being heard nor considered.

Local, county, state or federal politics . . . its up to you. Participation by public protest, a write-in campaign, or via an internet petition are all also game. We've seen the Tea Party and the Occupy Movement. We've seen major websites shut down to protest the SOPA law (Stop Online Privacy Act). We've also seen calls to write to our Senators and Congressmen to support or object to various legislation that come up for vote.

Above all else, its important to vote. Though the debate rages on as to whether our votes really count, when you take no action at all, you guarantee the exclusion of your vote. Now more than ever, we need everyone participating in the system, as our elected officials continue to forget that they are there to represent we the people, and not the other way around.

Take 5: The Story of D Black

The Story, by Abdul Majid

In 2010 I get a phone call one night from my boy D Black who lives out in Houston, Texas. He's all excited because he just met some fine ass woman when he was out the other night, and had a story to tell me . . . and his stories are always great.

So now let me tell you a little something about D Black before I continue with this anecdote. I've known D Black for over 21 years. He and I met my freshman year in high school when I was living in Pasadena, California and we've been friends ever since. He is my best friend on the planet and probably one of the nicest, smartest, funniest people I've ever met . . . . and D Black is a whore. He refers to him self as "The most eligible married man in America" (did I forget to mention he was married), so that should give you a little insight into his relationships with women.

So he calls me up all excited to tell me about last night festivities.

Me
D what up?

D Black
Shit, you know what it is.

Me
Same soup just reheated?

D Black
Pretty much . . . . Ay yo I called to tell you about this banging ass bitch I went out with the other night.

Me
God damn nigga another one?

D Black
Nigga I had to. This bitch was fine than a motherfucka. Body like a race track and built for speed.

Me
So did you hit?

D Black
Nigga did I! I beat them draws up like Tyson off his medication!

Me
Ha ha ha ha!!!!! So where'd you go cuz I know you didn't take her back to your place?

D Black
No sir, we went back to her place and had good ole barbecue.

Me
(Confused)
A barbecue?

D Black
Hell yeah nigga, cuz by the end of the night it
was my meat in her grill!

*If you're a woman please avoid this nigga at all
cost!!!!*

**"If you want a happy ending, that depends of
course on where you stop your story".—Orson
Welles.**

The Life Lesson, by James LeGrand

Fidelity is essential if our marriages and long-term
relationships are going to work.

We all have a choice to make. Do we want to be
in a loving, long-term and committed relationship,
or do we want to remain single, involved in much
shorter-term relationships and adventures. When
we make the decision to be involved in one or the
other, we are usually fine and happy to live with
the benefits and consequences of those decisions.
It's when we choose both without including our
mate in the decision that we create trouble for
ourselves.

A person in a marriage or committed long-term relationship has the reasonable expectation for a monogamous relationship. When one person is found to not be monogamous, it is the end of that relationship as you once knew it, regardless of whether you decide to officially end it or venture forward. Tied to the expectation of monogamy is trust, commitment, and the desire to keep the sanctity of that relationship sacred. If that is not your intent, then this relationship model is not for at this point in your life.

There is also nothing wrong with wanting to be single and involved with different partners at different times, provided you are honest about your intentions up front. As a single person, there is no expectation of monogamy. You can choose to do what you want, with whom you want, when you want, provided they are consenting.

Not everyone is ready for a long-term relationship. Also, not everyone wants to be single forever. For most of us, we have to make the decision for ourselves for when we are ready to move from a single lifestyle to a committed life style. Its more about knowing for ourselves when its time to move from one to the other. We just have to make sure we consider the thoughts and feelings of others as we make our decisions. Also, once we make the decision to commit, we should seek to honor that commitment for ourselves and those we are committed to.

Take 6: This Pimp I Know

The Story, by Abdul Majid

Back in 2000 while out at an album release party at the China Club, I met and became friends with this pimp named G Money (yes nigga, a 100%, thorough breed, where's my money bitch, pimp, pimp). Now I didn't know he was a pimp, hence the reason for me telling this story. He told me he was a talent manager for this all girl group and at the time I was booking musical acts for a television show called "The Daily Beat" so we started to talk.

Well one day I'm leaving the office really late on 8th Avenue between 34th and 35th and headed to the Port Authority Bus Terminal on 42nd and 8th to catch the last bus to Elizabeth, New Jersey. The 112 bus dropped me off closer to my apartment in Elizabeth than the train did, but as I'm leaving the office it starts to rain like cats and dogs. Now I'm in a rush, but my dumb ass didn't bring an umbrella even though the forecast said chance of rain. So now I'm not only getting soaked because I don't have an umbrella, I'm steady trying to duck the rain by going from awning to awning of the local delis on 8th Avenue looking like a fool in the process (like I give a shit).

Underneath one of the awnings, I hear a car horn honk and someone screaming my name. I look over and it was G Money in his brand new Mercedes Benz s500 asking me if I needed a ride. Now I know it seems a little questionable for a nigga to honk at you and you go running to a car, especially in New York, but all I could think was "rain, car, rain, car?" Of course I said yes and took the ride.

As he's driving me to the bus terminal, he gets a call from one of his "Artist", puts the call on speaker phone, and during the conversation I started to get a sneaking suspicion that he was the genuine article, live in the flesh pimp and she could possible be one of his whores, if not his bottom bitch . . . This should be interesting.

G Money
What it do?

Possible Whore
Hey daddy

G Money
Where you at bitch?

Possible Whore
Sitting in some raggedy ass diner.

G Money
What the fuck you doin' sitting in a diner? You ain't gonna make me my money that way. Bitch you better get off your ass and get me my bread.

Possible Whore
But my feet hurt daddy. Can I have just like 30
more minutes?

G Money
Bitch if I got to get out of this car and come to
that diner I'ma put my goon hand on you and
comb your muthfuckin forehead back.

Possible Whore
But daddy it's raining.

G Money
Bitch I don't care if it's raining razor blades. You'd
better get me my money . . . . and you'd better
not get cut.

*At that point my suspicions were correct and the
Possible Whore turned into an Actual Whore.*

You teach people how to treat you.

The Life Lesson, by James LeGrand

Ladies, your self-esteem is one of your most
prized possessions. Don't give it to those that will
take advantage of it to abuse you.

This story makes the abuse a fragile self-esteem
is willing to endure obvious, and the ridiculous
lengths a damaged person will go through to please

her abuser. However, if you are in a physically or verbally abusive relationship, is it any better? You deserve better than that. It is your self-esteem that is your internal gauge that determines what you believe you deserve and what you are willing to tolerate.

If you are in a relationship that works to tear down your self esteem, that's a relationship to run from. Those that love and care about you will seek only to build you up. So, what are you willing to endure? What do you think you deserve?

Determine your self worth for yourself. Only you can truly make that determination. Just remember that you were born valuable, and no one can take that away from you. Then, remove people from your life that work to tear you down and include people in your life that will work to build up your confidence. Then, seek the life you deserve, and don't stop until you've created it. It all starts and ends with you.

Take 7: Father Knows Best

The Story, by Abdul Majid

I have to start this story off by saying I absolutely love my father. He is my hero, I respect him tremendously and he is one of my two favorite people on the planet (my mother being the other even though she past away in '02). As a man he is probably one of the most intelligent people I've come across bar none. His analytical skills and critical thinking ability is comparable to that of Friedrich Nietzsche or Ayn Rand, so it is no surprise that I go to him when I need a second opinion or just some good ole fatherly advice.

That being said, having a story entitled "Ignorance is Contagious" and my father being the principle of this particular story feels a bit awkward to tell . . . . but they say the apple don't fall that far from the tree so I'm sure that nigga will understand.

Several years back I wrote a script that was being optioned by a studio (who will remain nameless) which actually got picked up (but then they shelved the shit, but hey that's the game right) and I was extremely anxious about the outcome. Now being a writer is unlike most other art forms. It can be an extremely long, arduous and lonely road. You're constantly stuck in your own head culling for the right words or phrases to use, and the process of having to wait for other people to read your work then respond back to you can make even the most cocksure person a little ambivalent about their abilities.

So I called my father (who is normally a sage) looking for some reassurance through his humorous words of wisdom like only he can provide. But on that day, he must have been tapping into his inner nigga because this is what I got.

My Father
Hey what's happening chief?

Me
You know, same ole same ole.

My Father
You sound a little down. What's the problem?

Me
It's nothing big. It's just . . . . I'm waiting for this fucking studio to call me back and it's taking forever.

My Father
Just be patient brotha. All good things come to those who wait. I bet you'd rather have this problem then not?

Me
I guess you're right about that.

My Father
To be honest with you, what you really should be worried about is what's about to come next.

Me
What do you mean?

My Father
The movie business is a dirty game. You know the grass ain't always greener on the other side. Sometimes it's brown . . . . and that's from them niggas pissing on it.

I'm sitting there thinking to myself "For real son? Like seriously nigga? That's the best you got for me?" . . . But oddly enough after everything went down he was absolutely correct . . . because in this industry, if you give them a chance they will try to piss on your dreams.

"I believe that what we become depends on what our fathers teach us at odd moments when they aren't trying to teach us."—Umberto Eco

The Life Lesson, by James LeGrand

Fathers, its time to reclaim our role in society for the children we bring into this world.

Too many men are walking away from their children. This is a trend that is growing across all cultures, and is especially prevalent in African American families. While many of our marriages and long-term relationships are ending, it does not mean that our role as a father has ended as well. We must step up, step in, and make our presence felt. It is critical.

Fathers represent the first strong male role model in our lives. When it's present, boys have a model to grow into and girls have a model of what a quality man is for their life. When the father role is not present, our children seek it out in others, often outside of the family, and the first strong male role model is left up to chance.

When we grow up with our fathers, our respect for them allows them to have that ability to say things in a way that is deeply impactful without forcing it upon us. When they aren't present during our childhood, we often either fear them or have diminishing respect for them. We then assign that role to others to fill, for better or for worse.

Dads, its time to lead. You impact your children's lives much more than you know whether you are present or not. Why not make the positive impact of your presence felt? Why not teach them, and show them how to find their happiness? Single mothers do an incredible job of raising their children. Think of how much better things would be for your children if single mother's didn't have to fill the role of Dad as well.

Get in your children's lives and stay there.

Take 8: The Learning

The Story, by Abdul Majid

If you know me or have read any of my stories you'd know that I have a tendency to be very sarcastic, quick witted and have a wry sense of humor (which pretty much means I talk a lot of shit). Well this endearing character trait of mine didn't come by over night. It has taken years of cultivating to achieve this high level of assholeness and I must regrettably say that my poor mother being the first line of defense in our household would bear the brunt of my "cultivation".

My mother (god bless her soul) was a very beautiful half Chinese and half Panamanian woman that was born and raised in Colón, Panama. Now even though she was bilingual and English was her 2nd language, her English was spot on without even a hint of an accent. Every now and again her translation of a word would get mixed up and me being the little shit that I was/am, I WOULD GO IN (regardless of the consequences).

See, the thing about my mother and I would assume it goes for all good mothers, is that a crucial part of their nurturing spirit comes from patience. For a mother, patience will turn her possible murder charge into a scolding and a guilt trip. But, at a certain point even mother Teresa will lose her cool and her patience will turn into frustration, which will eventually turn you into a patient (In-patient or outpatient, it depends on how hard you push those buttons).

Now in the early 80's in the tri-state area at noon on channel 5 they would show these kung fu movies and my family loved, loved, loved, kung fu movies. From the Shaw Brothers movies to Golden Harvest productions, it was like a family tradition that every Saturday my father, mother, brother, two sisters and I would sit in front of the television and would watch these kung fu movies. It always seems that for me that my greatest family memories never happen in some overt, grandiose gesture but during some little ordinary life occurrence.

On this particular Saturday my father had to work, my brother was out on a boating trip and my two sisters were upstairs at a neighbor's house, so that pretty much gave me carte blanche to act an ass. Well my mother and I are sitting next to each other on the couch watching this kung fu movie, which I believe was call the "Cripple Avengers" (which is fitting for this story) when I start jumping up and down on the couch doing my kung fu moves, annoying the shit out of my mother.

My Mother
Boy if you don't act like you got some sense and stop jumping on my damn couch.

Me
No but look . . . . I'm Hung See Kwon like in the
movie. Key ya, key ya!

My Mother
(Annoyed)
Just because your father's not here doesn't
mean you can act any ole way want to.

Me
(Mumbling)
Whatever.

My Mother
Keep talking back and I'ma learn you a lesson.

Me
(Sarcastically)
Learn you? That ain't even a word.

My Mother
Neither is this.

AND SHE STRAIGHT SLAPPED ME THE FUCK
OFF THE COUTCH!!!!

My Mother
(Continued)
Now Hung See Kwon that.

Listen to your mother!

"In the vain laughter of folly wisdom hears half its applause."—George Eliot (pseudonym for Mary Anne Evans)

The Life Lesson, by James LeGrand

From childhood through adulthood and old age, always respect your parents.

As children, our parents take care of us and teach us many of the skills and philosophies that help us to grow and find success. As young adults, they can be sources of great advice, needed emotional support, and love when we don't feel that love from others. In their older age, the roles reverse as they count on us to be there for them, ensure their comfort, and to help them make sense of a long life that is nearing its end.

Many people have unresolved issues with our parents from childhood. It's important to realize that they were doing the best they could with what they knew and what they had. If they knew better or were capable of more, they would have done better or provided more. To properly heal your relationships with your parents, take the responsibility for the relationship, determine what changes you need to make to fix the relationship in your mind, and begin anew. Remember that you cannot force anyone outside of yourself to change.

It's also important to remember that one of the best gifts you can give your parents is your independence. It not only becomes a great source of pride for your parents, but it also frees them up to live their lives without people continuing to be a financial and energetic drain on their lives. In living a financial and emotional independent life, we are freeing our parents from the responsibility of caring for us, while at the same time preparing our lives to assist them.

Take 9: Choking On BIG Smoke

The Story, by Abdul Majid

I am constantly being asked if I do drugs because of some of the left field shit that come out of my head, and the answer in an emphatic NO. But I would be remiss if I didn't say I partook in the cannabis sativa once or twice in my life, and back in '93 I smoked that ooh wee for the very first time.

While at home in Scotch Plains, New Jersey (yeah I moved around a lot) I get a call from my boy Eric who wanted to know if I wanted to go to this free concert in the Bronx, and me being the nigga that I am all I heard was free and jumped on that shit quick as hell. Eric and I became friends back in the 8th grade (in the 11th now) at Hubbard Middle School in Plainfield, New Jersey. We use to go back and forth reciting all of our favorite rap lyrics during gym class and on the playground at lunch time (and I was nice with mine son, ask around).

So knowing my affinity for rap music he told me that Fat Joe was having a concert at the Skate Key in the Bronx . . . all we had to do was help set up and we could watch the show for free. So he picks me up in his blue Volvo and off we go to the Bronx (where he's originally from) like two bandits on a mission.

After a little bit of traffic on the New Jersey Turnpike and George Washington Bridge we finally arrive at the Skate Key in true nigga fashion, late as all hell. We go inside but by that time all the manual labor had been done, so we fronted like we did some work and got to stay for the show (score 1 for the two lazy niggas from Jersey). After being inside for about 10 minutes or so, Eric sees his friend whose name I can't remember (insert weed joke here) and makes a bee line towards him.

He introduces me to his friend who we'll just call "The Provider" and after a quick meet and greet (a dap and a what's good) he gives Eric the look. The Provider whose brother, cousin or friend was promoting the event scored some weed and decided he wanted to bless his little homie with a bit of the herb for doing such a bang up job. The Provider being such a gregarious person decides he doesn't want to smoke alone and asked if we'd like to partake in a session. Eric who obviously smoked (because his extra black lips told the tale) agreed but being a smoke virgin, I decided to decline. After a bit of coercion, compounded by the fact that I didn't want to be known as "that lame ass nigga from Jersey" after I left the Bronx,

I agreed to join in the session (peer pressures a bitch).

To be completely honest with you, it didn't take that much arm twisting. A quick exchange with The Providers and him saying something about it being natural and from the erff (yes nigga with two F's) and it was a go. Eight and a half minutes later we're parked on some side street in the Bronx, Eric in the driver's seat, The Provider riding shotgun with me in the back waiting for the L to be rolled. The Provider does the honors being that it is his stash then sparks the L to start the session and the chiefing begins.

Now I don't claim to be an expert so I don't know what the exact nomenclature is for this particular brand of marijuana, but that shit had us high as giraffe ass quickly. All of a sudden The Provider being the philosophical academician he is decides he wants to start up a conversation.

The Provider
Yo this L got me right son.

Eric
You ain't never lie.

Me
(With my corny ass)
Word

The Provider

Yo I was thinking. You ever been like high and watching cartoons like Bugs Bunny and shit and your dick get harder than Chinese arithmetic?

Me
(In the back concerned)
WHAT!?!

Eric
Nah son.

The Provider
(Defensive)
Nah, nah, nah, not on some faggot shit . . . . but like some of them shits be sexy as hell. I was watching Looney Tunes the other night and that motherfuckin pig was dressed like a little Indian bitch . . . . Yo Porky Pig got a fat ass son!

And that was the beginning of my sobriety . . . with a few relapses in between . . . read on.

Drugs are bad . . . **Just Say No!**

The Life Lesson, by James LeGrand

The United States, and elsewhere around the world, is becoming more and more of a drug culture. Whether we are talking about illegal drugs, over the counter drugs, caffeine, nicotine or even sugar, we as a culture turn to drugs or other things that alter our state of being more and more. Unfortunately, what we gain in terms of relaxation or taking our mind off of our troubles temporarily, we lose in the impact on our ability to make decisions, to analyze and to react. In addition, the potential to find ourselves hooked on a particular substance is always of concern.

Today, individuals use these drugs and other addictive substances for entertainment, to escape from their problems, to be a part of the "in" crowd, or because they are already addicted and believe they need it to function. It's important that we let go of our relationship with drugs and accept a trust and harmony within ourselves that we can function better without them.

Personally speaking, I've never attempted marijuana or other illegal drugs, and I have only taken an over the counter drug of any kind 5 times since 1985 (2 Tylenol after a nasty dehydration headache in the late 1990's, 2 muscle relaxers during my honeymoon after straining a muscle in my neck after horseback riding in 2009, and 1 Aleve after tweaking my back after moving some very heavy boxes in 2010). As a teenager in the 1980's I saw first hand the growing drug culture in other teenagers and in adults, and I made a conscious decision to not participate in any way.

While I know most people won't be as extreme as I am with drug avoidance (even over the counter), I believe there is benefit in moving towards more natural means of reducing stress, headaches and dealing with problems. In doing so, when you really need a particular over the counter drug for medical reasons, it is more likely to actually work. The other benefits are clarity of mind, the development of healthy coping mechanisms, and better physical health.

Take 10: The Role Model

The Story, by Abdul Majid

On December 1, 2001 I got laid of from a television job I truly loved and the post 9/11 economic times being what they were, I had a hard time obtaining another full time job. So I started freelancing. If you've ever been a freelancer or know anyone who has, you'd know that it can be a touch and go job at times and the process of getting paid takes a little while. So I took a part time job working at the YMCA in Elizabeth, NJ in the fitness center as a personal trainer (respect my sexy) to supplement my income.

Now at most YMCA's along with a gym and basketball court there is an after school program as well. This particular YMCA was no different and working in this after school program I met a delightful character by the name of Keyshawn (the names are changed to protect the ignorant). In a word Keyshawn is a nigga, and is proud of it. He is the walking, talking embodiment of what a nigga is. His morals, beliefs, values, philosophies, ideologies and all around disposition is that of a nigga.

Elizabeth, New Jersey is a predominantly African American and Latino community so it is no coincidence that this after school program would have the same ethnic make up. But every now and again you'd have a couple of white kids peppered into the group. The white kid in this group was named Bobby (not his real name) along with his mother Pam (not her real name). Bobby and Pam on a genetic level are Caucasian (I'm talking peas in the potato salad, straight from the Caucasus Mountains, white, white), but if you took a glimpse at their wardrobe or listened to their speaking patterns you'd know that those two were some niggas.

Pam was a semi attractive, slightly over weight woman who you could tell from that look in her eyes had a predilection for the spice meat (mostly sausage). Like a peacock flaunting her feathers, Pam had every accoutrement available to catch herself a nigga male. From the Baby Phat designer clothing she wore (or whatever was fashionable at the time) to the finely coiffed hair and silk wrapped, French tipped, manicured nails (with the hieroglyphic shit on it). Now if you know niggas like I know niggas you'd know that it is every male nigga's dream to get himself a "white girl" (for their credit if not for the tax benefits alone) and Keyshawn was no exception. One look at this Aryan princess and Keyshawn was hooked and tried his best on numerous occasions to get her attention, but to no avail.

On this particular day I was putting away some basketballs (no joke needed) in a storage closet in a room that acted as a make shift lunchroom for the kids in the after school program. I walk into the room while the kids were beginning to eat their snacks when Keyshawn sees me and comes over to say "What's up". Now it being snack time, most of the children were eating crackers, chips or fruit, but not Bobby. Being a little nigga in training, Bobby had himself a snack box. If you don't know what a snack box is you should go down to your local chicken shack in any ghetto U.S.A and for $3.50 you can pick up one for yourself. It consists of two pieces of fried chicken, French fries, a roll and a C&C soda (the nigga beverage of choice, ask for it by name).

Now fried chicken to a nigga is an aphrodisiac. It's like some southern fried pheromone and Keyshawn being the quintessential nigga locked on to the scent like a hound dog. His nostrils turned into a homing device and he located the whereabouts of that yard bird like Doppler radar. Seeing that it was Bobby, the son of his favorite Caucasian and would be sponsor, he made his way over to try and ingratiate himself to the boy.

Keyshawn
Hey little man

Bobby
Hey Mr. Keyshawn

Keyshawn
What you eatin' there, some chicken?

Bobby
Mmm hmm

Keyshawn
You tearin' it up too, ain't chu boy?

Bobby
It's good.

Keyshawn
Look at chu, got your Sean John jeans on and your Jordan sneakers . . . looking all clean . . . I swear if you ain't a nigga you play one on TV.

I fell the fuck out!!! Although I heard later his mother wasn't too pleased by his compliment.

Not everyone is qualified to be someone's role model. Be cautious of the people you follow.

The Life Lesson, by James LeGrand

Now more than ever, we need quality role models.

We live in an age of broken families, of absent parents who manage their kids instead of raising them, and of consistently negative environments. In order to sell their products, television tells us that we are not good enough and therefore need whatever they are selling to feel better about our selves. Our families sometime tell us that we are wrong to pursue our dreams, because they were afraid to pursue theirs. Sometimes, a child can hear good advice better if it came from someone outside of the family so that they believe the advice is sincere.

Whatever the circumstance, we need more quality role models. So what makes a quality role model? First, one must walk the walk. It's hard to follow someone who gives advice on your life while their life is in shambles. Quality role models have lives that others want to "model" themselves after. Also, quality role models understand that their "role" in a child's life is to lead by example, to provide encouragement, and to provide suggestions for the person they are coaching so they have good information to make decisions on.

When a role model has an ulterior motive, such as in the story above, they are insincere, using the child for their own potential gain, and setting up a circumstance that will make it more difficult for that child to trust again in the future. If this is what you are doing, you will make the world a better place by not pretending to be a role model.

Get your life together, be a great example that is worthy of following, then share your story, advice and wisdom to kids that can benefit from it.

Take 11: The Chronicles of the Bitches: The Whore, The Slut and The Scumbag

The Story, by Abdul Majid

Okay, now I know what you're thinking. Having read the title of this story or perused through some of my previous works and learned a little bit about my upbringing you're probably saying to yourself "I know your parents taught you better than to be calling woman bitches" or "How dare you castigate these woman with such vitriol and vituperation". Now before you render judgments from the title alone please allow me to finish the story, and then you can decide for yourself.

In early 2000, I got a call from a music producer friend of mine named Bless while I was at work. He and his partner K Mack are a production team called "The Soul Diggaz" and were going to be at Sony recording studios on 54th street between 9th and 10th working on some music and said if I were going to be in the area that I should come through. Being that I worked on 8th Ave between 34 and 35 and it was only a hop, skip and a jump away, I decided to drop by.

Arriving at the studio around 11 o'clock, I was buzzed into the building then informed by the front desk receptionist that they were in studio "B" and I could just walk on back when ready. As I walked down the hallway I passed studio "A" and exiting the studio was an A&R executive friend of mine and a female associate of his. After exchanging hugs and pounds I tell him why I'm there and he tells me to come by when I was done so we could chop it up for a minute (talk).

Now fast forward to 2 A.M; while Bless and K Mack are working on a mix with an engineer. I decide to take a walk down the hall and pop my head in (no homo) to say "What's up" to my boy. As I open the door to the studio I have to walk past three women sitting on a couch in the lounge in order to get to the control room door. I enter the control room and see that my A&R friend, the rap artist he's working with and the rappers entourage are all having a chiefing session to what I'm assuming was an attempt to get the rappers mind right so that he can spit those super dope lyrics about bitches, guns and narco trafficking (you know the song).

The A&R sees me and asks me if I want in on this session, but as you should already know from my previous story, I don't smoke weed (anymore) so I decline. After a few minutes of being in this smoke filled room the smoke begins to bother me (temptation) and I told my A&R friend that I'm going to chill in the lounge for a while and when he's done to come out and holla at me.

Upon entering the lounge I take a seat next to these 3 gorgeous women (gotta give credit where credit's due) who just happen to be gold digging, blood sucking leeches (gotta give credit where credit's due). Now if you know anything about this brand of women you'd know that if you are a person of note (ballers, brawlers, and shot callers), they are the most affable, engaging, and charismatic women you could ever meet. On the other hand if they consider you an all so ran, they treat you as if were infected with lame ass nigga disease and will ignore the shit out of you.

As I sat there they treated me as the latter and they began to completely ignore me. Me being the astute observer of human behavior that I am just sat back, listened intently and took mental notes on their conversation. Now normally I'm not one to cast dispersion on any ones weltanschauung (look it up) or physical drawbacks, but these bitches had to either have been suffering from some type of optical defect or getting a contact high from the marijuana smoke coming in from the other room if they couldn't see how god damn fine I was (nigga I'm man pretty) . . . . but I digress.

Anyway, they began to talk about their trip to the 2004 NBA All Star Weekend and which one of their financiers would bear the cost of this trip.

Whore
So are you two going shopping with me tomorrow?

Slut
For what?

Whore
I need so new clothes for Cali.

Scumbag
No, I'ma go a couple days earlier and just go shopping out there.

Whore
Is "famous basketball player" taking you shopping out there?

Scumbag
I'm not going with him.

Slut
Then who the fuck are you going with?

Whore
For real, talk about it.

Scumbag
I'm done fucking with "famous basketball player". "Famous rapper" is taking me.

Whore
Why you still fucking with "famous rapper"? He ain't got no real money.

Scumbag
What you ain't hear? He just signed his deal with (Big Record Label) . . . . shiiiiiiit, don't sleep on my skills. I can smell a check from a mile away.

"And you wonder why they call you bitch?" Tupac

Don't be fooled by the allure and find yourself a person of good moral character. If you settle down with the wrong person, you will curse the day you met that raggedy bitch . . . . **ask around!!!**

The Life Lesson, by James LeGrand

Men and women . . . beware of the users.

There are people out there whose full time job is to take from you what they believe they cannot get for themselves. They do this by getting into your life, artificially pumping up your ego, and then slowly getting you to want to do what they want you to do. They are masters of manipulation and influence. Once they lock on to you, you'll never have a more fun time losing the house to them.

In this story, the targets are typically wealthy. Actors and musicians have to deal with groupies all the time, and to some degree, there is a mutual usury taking place in those industries. For the every day person, however, these people normally sneak into your life without your knowledge that they are after what you have and not who you are.

Understand that you are not your car, your house, your career, your money, or anything that lies outside of yourself. When your self-esteem is based on any of these things, you are an easy target. These users will pump up your ego around whatever you believe defines you, get you to trust them, get you to fall for them, slowly extract whatever they can from you, and when there is nothing left, they dump you.

What's interesting is that at first, they aren't taking anything . . . . you find yourself wanting to give things to them. They convince you that they care about you. They ensure you have a great time with them. Then over time, they go from accepting your gifts, to hinting to things they would like so you can "surprise" them, to outright stating what they want with the expectation you will get it for them.

If you want to avoid these users, start with strengthening your own self-esteem and anchoring it who you are on the inside, and not on what you have. Then, listen to your intuition when it tells you that something is strange in the relationship.

People have a way of telling you who they are right up front, so look for those indications. When you find that you are with a user, break off contact, and end it before it becomes something more to you. It's for your own good and protection.

Take 12: Good Lovin' Body Rockin' Knockin' Boots All Night Long

The Story, by Abdul Majid

I was having a conversation with a friend of mine named Eugene Grayer a couple of weeks ago about how all these young kids are having sex at an early age and it got me to thinking about the time I lost my virginity. I was 18 years old and a senior at Scotch Plains Fanwood High School when I decided to take on the monumental task of finding a person I could connect with on a spiritual level (I'm just bullshitting I just wanted some ass).

Now no disrespect to all my snow bunnies out there, but growing up I was feed a steady diet of The Cosby Show, A Different World, and R&B and Rap music videos. For my first sexual experience, all I wanted was that pretty brown round (It's driving me wild). Scotch Plains being a majority Caucasian community did not give the optimal environment to get that chocolate goodness I was desperately searching for. Me being the adventurous soul that I was I ventured one town over to Plainfield, New Jersey which was a predominantly African American community to continue my vision quest.

As you all know from my "Choking on big smoke" story, I went to Hubbard Middle school in the 8th grade so I knew a few people who could introduce me to a few things to get this party started. Trying for months to get a "Sista" who would be down to do that dance and play this game we call love was more difficult then I imaged. Never the quitter, in a last ditch effort I called a friend, who had a friend, who had someone they wanted to introduce me to (say that 3 times fast).

On a Tuesday (I think it was) I went by my friend's place to meet this girl and what I saw wasn't exactly what I was looking for. See, god has an incredible sense of humor and he will test you to see how much you want what it is you say you want. What was presented to me was pretty, but it was neither brown nor round. Just my luck I get the only white girl in all of fucking Plainfield, who for the sake of the story we'll call Door #1.

Door #1 was a very nice, pretty girl (who was into the spice meat) with a nice rack (like most snow bunnies have), but the hind quarters? . . . well they were exactly that . . . quarters (shiny and flat). This being last chance saloon for me (or at least that's what I thought) I proceeded to blandish her with attention and adulation. After courting her for several weeks, the day I had been praying for had finally arrived. After school on a

Thursday she stopped by my house to hangout with me for a while, like we've done on several occasions. Unbeknownst to me, hanging out that day meant something completely different (like my balls nigga).

When she arrived, my stepmother answered the door, lets her in, then called me down to tell me I had company. I come down and tell my stepmother that we're going upstairs to "study," then I escort Door #1 to my bedroom. After a few minutes of the normal conversation and the necessary jibber jabber the make out session begins. Doing all those things you do to get to the point of getting laid, I figured this would be my best chance to test the waters. I do my patented and world-renowned drop draws move, but was halted by her concerns about my stepmother being down stairs and my older brother in the next room. At this point I'm harder than Chinese arithmetic so I give her some bullshit ass line about them going to the store in a few (you do what you gotta do) and the session continues.

So I lock my bedroom door, strap up and we start to do the horizontal mambo like only two teenagers could do. Now my ego would love to tell you that I beat them draws up into a comatose-like blissful submission, but that wasn't even close to being the case. Nigga I two-pump chumped that bitch so fast it was like I was trying to break an Olympic record. I'm not even sure she broke a sweat, was an active participant or even aware of what was going on. For those several glorious seconds

I humped her brains out like a wild monkey screaming and shrieking the whole time.

Now in my defense it was my first time and things like that happen on your first time at anything (practice makes perfect), because I know as an adult I can sling that loaf something ridiculous (and it is a loaf ladies). After our enjoyable, but brief sexual encounter was over, the inevitable post sex conversation took place.

Door #1
So that's it?

Me
Yeah pretty much that's what I'm going with.

Door #1
Oh

Me
Why, what's up?

Door #1
Nothing . . . . but I'm just curious. Was that your first time?

Me
(Embarrassed)
First time?

Door #1
Yeah, having sex.

Me
(Embarrassed as hell)
Ummmm . . . . I roughed up the suspect a couple
times . . . . does that count?

*I make fun of everyone else so much I figured my
time was due. Enjoy!!!*

**All jokes aside, your virginity is a special thing
so guard it well and only give it to the right
person.**

The Life Lesson, by James LeGrand

It's difficult to talk about your first time, but it's
easy to learn lessons from it.

For most of us, it's cloaked in awkwardness at
best, and shame at worse. However, there are
some key things we can learn from this life altering
experience.

For those who have not yet had their first time,
first, be sure you are ready. Don't do it because all
of your friends said they have done it (especially
true of boys). I fell into this trap personally. I thought
I was the last in my group of friends. It was only
when I had my first time that I discovered I was
one of the first amongst my friends. I really wasn't
ready, and I knew it. Trust me, when everyone
says they've had their first time in high school, they
probably haven't. Don't do it due to peer pressure.

If you do decide to venture forth, make sure it is for your own reasons and in your own time.

Whether you've yet to have your first time or you have decades of experience, do use protection with each encounter. For some, that protection comes in the form of a committed and monogamous relationship. For others, that protection comes in the form of a condom. However you choose to protect yourself, think about how to remain disease free, how not to spread any diseases you have, and how to not bring children into the world until you are ready to do so.

Take 13: Duke The Moon

The Story, by Abdul Majid

On December 28, 2008 I turned the ripe old age of 33. So like I've been doing since I turned 26, after the New Year I scheduled a doctors appointment for my biannual checkup. When I called to make an appointment, unbeknownst to me the doctor I regularly go to decided to switch hospitals and I was left doctorless. Now most of you may not know this, but I come from a family of doctors (on my mothers side mostly) so it was nothing for me to get a referral for another doctor.

My cousin who works in the emergency room at Columbia Presbyterian Hospital in New York City gave me a referral to one of his colleagues who is suppose to be an amazing doctor at this hospital. I call, make the appointment and in a few weeks I'm off to get my check up. Having never met or spoken to this woman before I was pleasantly surprised that she was a very attractive, late 30's, Spanish woman and for the sake of this story we'll call her Dr. Culo Dedo. We exchange pleasantries and a quick story about how we both knew my cousin then it was off to the physical.

She takes my blood pressure (88/56), my resting heart rate (69 bpm), then she draws blood to test my HDL and LDL level, to check my insulin level, test for STD's and whatever the hell else they needed it for. Lastly (or so I think), she did the dreaded Q-tip swab in the penis for the Gonorrhea/Chlamydia test (and I'm happy to say that I'm as clean as the board of health and have the papers to prove it).

So I pull up my pants thinking that my physical was over, but she tells me to stop. Having done this type of physical many times before, I immediately asked her why. She says that I have one more test to do and it requires me to have my pants down. I say half joking with my pants around my ankles and my hands on my hips (like in a superman pose), "Now what test would that be," and then I gave her a wink. She looks at me with a smile and says "Your prostate cancer screening," and then gives me a wink back.

I already knew exactly what that entailed and I responded with a quick "You must be out of yo fucking mind. I'm only 33 and I don't even let people wave their finger in my face". She said because my mother had breast cancer and my father had pre-cancerous colon polyps, I ran a higher chance of having cancer and it would be wise of me to have it checked at an earlier age then the suggested age of 40. Still defiant I said, "Hell no," and started buckling my belt.

All of a sudden she starts to ramble off all the statistics imaginable like "Did you know that black males run a higher rate of colon cancer then any other race," "Blacks as a whole are more likely to get cancer than any other race," and this and that and 9 out of 10 dentist prefer Crest and blah, blah, blah. I was so mesmerized by all the information being thrown at me that the next thing you know I was bent over a table (no homo) with my pants at my ankle and my ass to the wind.

So she slaps on some latex gloves, puts on whatever the ass lubricant they use on her left index finger and I know this just might have been my imagination but I could have sworn she called me a bitch and chuckled under her breath. I take three quick breaths and then it's on.

Dr. Culo Dedo
This will just take a second.

Me
(Breathing heavy and grimacing)
Please hurry up.

Dr. Culo Dedo
I'm trying but I need you to relax.

Me
(Breathing heavy and grimacing)
I am relaxed!

Dr. Culo Dedo
No you're not Mr. Majid. Now I need for you to take a deep breath and unclench my finger.

Me
(Breathing heavy and grimacing)
I'm trying . . . . but I think my ass locked up.

I'm happy to inform you that I was given a clean bill of health.

An ounce of prevention is worth a pound of cure.

The Life Lesson, by James LeGrand

It is important that we all take responsibility for our health and healthcare.

Far too many of us drop our bodies off to a doctor every now and then, as if we are dropping our cars off to an auto mechanic, and then expect the doctor to hand our bodies back all bright and shiny again. The doctor is not responsible for our healthcare. Nor is our insurance company, parents, spouse, or children. The buck starts and ends with us.

Healthcare starts at home. The foods you eat, the things you drink, the types and frequency of your exercise, and the amount of sleep you get are all key factors in your healthcare. Yet, we allow ourselves to eat things that can only loosely be defined as food, we drink liquid sugar, we exercise our thumbs on the remote controls of our lives, and we get less and less sleep. If you want to see less of the doctor in your later years, you must take better care of yourself in your earlier years.

One of the most important decisions we can make is to control the food we eat, as it is a major factor in many of the healthcare problems we encounter (though not the only one). High blood pressure, heart disease, cancer, and diabetes can all be eliminated or greatly reduced with a change with our relationship with food. Obesity, which is steadily on the rise and is now affecting our children, can wreck havoc on our bodies, and yet, we allow this slow death to march on in our families, with our friends and within ourselves.

We've prioritized speed and convenience over quality and nutritional value when it comes to our food. We would rather have fast food than to go home and prepare a quality meal. We would rather use the microwave than to use the oven. We would rather fry than to bake, eat sodium packed foods than fresh foods, and eat sugar rich snacks and foods than healthier alternatives.

Our long-term and short-term goals will always conflict, so it's important to choose the long-term goals. Therefore, if long term you wish to live a healthy life, but short term, you want the #1 at your favorite restaurant, make the decision that is consistent with your long-term goals. Its right about now that someone says or thinks, "Easier said than done." That is the cop out of choice, which basically says that they will not even begin.

Of course it's easier said than done. All efforts worthy of time and energy are easier said than done. That doesn't mean you don't begin.

Make the choice today to control your own healthcare. See a doctor regularly. Conduct the screenings that make sense to do depending on where you are in life. Stop smoking complete, and limit your alcohol intake (or stop altogether). Drink plenty of water and reduce your soda and other sweet beverage intake. Cook more the old fashioned way . . . in the oven. Reduce your sugar snacks and increase your intake of fruits and vegetables.

As of this writing, I've been a vegetarian for 6 months to support a good friend in his quest to cure a rare form of cancer. Before his cancer, I never thought I could stick with a vegetarian lifestyle, and others who know me as the carnivore I've always been had their doubts as well. However, with my friend providing the spark, I became a vegetarian, and actually began to enjoy it. I lost 16 pounds (and I was in good shape), my energy went through the roof (and I was already pretty energetic), and I just felt better physically. It was easier said than done, yet I did it. I made the lifestyle change that allows me much better choices. I'm in no way saying that you should do this as well . . . merely that if I'm going to talk the talk, I too have to walk the walk. I'm walking. What new choice do you have to make to take control of your healthcare?

Take 14: 3 Niggas And A Wedding

The Story, by Abdul Majid

On June 20, 2009 at 3:30 pm EST, my oldes brother James LeGrand (co-author of this book) got married to his beautiful fiancé Christina in the Pocono Mountains in Pennsylvania. It always warms your heart to see a good, functioning relationship, because as a couple, these two are the most respectful, spiritual, hard working, loving couple you could ever meet and may god bless their union. That being said it got me thinking about what the antithesis to that type of relationship would be and it brings me to the point of this story.

I have a younger brother named Animal (not real name) and Animal shall we say is a little rough around the edges, a tad excitable and slightly uncouth (a Muslim nigga). So for the very first time in his life (adult of otherwise), he has fallen head over common sense in stone cold love. Now who do you ask is the person he is so enamored with? Well for his first shot at romance he picks a short, zaftig, fair skin woman (light skinded) by the name Yard Bird (not real name).

Like James and Christina, these two are also equally yoked but in a Bizzaro World, niggerish kind of way. From the Newports they smoke to the brown liquor they sip, these two motherfuckers are cut from the same cloth. I was always taught that two niggas are like similar matter and that they could not occupy the same space at the same time because they would ultimately destroy each other . . . . but these two have proven me wrong. I'm not sure if it's trust, faith, intestinal fortitude or just sheer stupidity, but somehow they make it work.

To call their relationship tumultuous would be an understatement and wouldn't even scratch the surface of the depth of this thing they call nigga love. Watching how they behaved is like watching fraternity brothers belittle and assault each other all in the name of brotherhood. To the untrained eyes and ears, listening to the way they speak to each other or watching their body language, you would think they didn't even like each other and for that matter are probably sworn enemies. The amount of vitriol and contempt they have for each other is tantamount to that episode of the Jerry Springer Show when Jerry went mano y mano with the grand dragon of the Ku Klux Klan (and you see how that turned out).

Now what compounds the hostility in this relationship is the fact that this is my brother's first true love. So if you've ever been head over common sense for a person, you'd know that it's like an open nerve that is constantly being touched . . . in the heat of the moment you don't always act in a rational manner. So on the day of the wedding my older brother Jubair and I were going to drive from Plainfield, New Jersey to the Pocono Mountains in Pennsylvania when all of a sudden I get a call from Animal.

Animal says that the windshield wipers on Yard Bird's car broke and that because of the rain they wanted to know if they could ride along with us to the wedding. I ask my brother Jubair who was driving if they could tag along, and his first impulse was to give me that "nigga are you out of your fucking mind" look. Then he immediately acquiesces because he knew what the right thing to do was. I call Animal back to tell him that they could come along when he tells me that Yard Bird's cousin who we'll call "Half A Tard" (Full Tard would just be disrespectful to retards around the world) also needed a ride to the wedding. I confer with Jubair who reluctantly gives them the green light (I think he yelled "FUCK!!!" first) and now the 3 of them are on their way.

As I stand outside awaiting their arrival, I see a white car in the distance driving towards the house with only the passenger side windshield wipers working and I immediately know it's them. They park in front of the house, pop the trunk open and my brother Animal hops out of the front passenger side of the car. He goes to the back of the car and starts to take some clothes out of the trunk because they decide to change clothes at the venue. Since it was raining, they didn't want to wrinkle their clothes while sitting in a car for two hours. Already irritated, I'm assuming because of the pouring rain or whatever nigga bullshit they got into (before, on the way to and while they were here), he pounds on the side of the car and yells.

Animal
(Yelling)
A yo, what the fuck you two waiting for, a motherfucking invitation? Get the fuck out the car! I swear y'all some simple yellow motherfuckas!

Nigga love, I swear it's a beautiful thing!!!!

You're nobody till somebody loves you.

The Life Lesson, by James LeGrand

Yes, this was my wedding! Though my wedding turned out to beautiful beyond our imagination, in addition to this story, we could easily bring up another four similar stories (perhaps in a follow up book), but this is a good one to focus on with respect to love relationships.

There are relationships for the short-term, relationships for the long-term, those you should avoid for now, and those you should always avoid.

With respect relationships for the short-term, know what you are looking for, be up front about it, and know that it cannot remain a short-term relationship for very long. Short-term relationships are those people that you date, they are the "friends with benefits", or the person or people you occasionally hook up with. Fun, excitement and compatible sexual energy are normally the requirements for these relationships.

However, eventually, they either get boring or they get serious. One way or the other, these relationships either end or change to a friendship or a long-term relationship. Be honest with yourself and your partner(s) about what you want, and when those desires change.

Long-term relationships should be reserved for the truly committed. If you plan to continue with short-term relationships, already see divorce in your future, or expect your partner to make major lasting changes for you, I recommend not getting involved in a long-term relationship.

Long-term relationships need more than love to work. Both parties need to be dedicated to partnership, fidelity, monogamy, compromise, have similar views on spirituality, have an understanding on their plans for children, and come to an agreement on how money will be managed within the relationship.

There are some relationships that you should avoid in the short-term. These are relationships with those that are going through significant emotional turmoil at the moment, those that recently ended a very serious long-term relationship, or those that you are not yet certain are where you are emotionally.

For these individuals, watch and wait. Make sure you know what you are getting involved in before you get involved. It's always easier to decide not to get into a relationship than it is to end one, so pay close attention in the early stages. People do tell on themselves right up front.

Then, there are the relationships you should just avoid at all costs. Anyone that is physically, verbally, or emotionally abusive is not going to be a good partner. If they hit you or threaten to hit you even once before you commit to them long-term, that is a sign of what is to come. Alcoholics, drug addicts, and child molesters, are all people to avoid at all costs for long-term relationships. Serial cheaters, people still in love with their ex's, and people who say, "if it doesn't work out, I'll just get a divorce" are all people to avoid for long-term relationships.

Relationships take a lot of work, so it's important to be honest with yourself and your partner(s). Break candidates down into these four groups, decide where you are within them, and then go for it. Just make sure that as you change, you alert the people around you of your evolution.

Take 15: A Drunken Mind Speaks A Sober Truth

The Story, by Abdul Majid

I was sitting at home on the computer (most likely on facebook) when I get a call from the sister of an old friend of mine who recently got out of jail. My friend the Penologist (not real name) and I went to elementary school together and I have to say in all honesty he is a really good guy, but even as a kid you could kind of tell that he was heading down that road.

Like most blacks living in a plebeian neighborhood where your opportunities are limited, self-esteem is damn near nonexistent and black male role models come few and far between. He like a lot of other black males started getting into trouble at an early age. Not having the greatest athletic abilities he did what most guys in that position did and started selling drugs (and got caught like most guys in his position).

Well as a kid I moved around a lot and after the third or fourth move we lost touch. One day while I was waiting for the train in Newark's Penn Station I ran into his sister and after a few minutes of chit chatting we exchanged numbers and said we'd keep in touch. On June 23, 2009 I get a call from his sister who surprises me by passing him the phone and after a 30-minute conversation, he asks me to come out to this bar in Newark so could have a drink and talk. As most of you know I don't drink but I went anyway just to catch up and shoot the shit with him.

I arrived at this bar early, which was situated in the middle of the block in this urban blight of a neighborhood and looked exactly like what you'd think an old 60's style run down bar would look like . . . broken windows, flickering light bulbs and all. It reminded me of that bar in the movie "Jackie Brown" when Jackie goes to talk to Ordell about how she's going to get him his money. By the way when Ordell said "Shit, Jackie, you come in this place on Saturday night I bet you need nigga repellant to keep motherfuckas off ya ass," it was probably one of the funniest lines I've heard thus far.

Anyway I go inside and take a seat two stools down from these two thuggish looking black men that were drinking Patron and having a conversation. Now as I'm watching the Jermaine Taylor fight on a flat screen TV, I can see out of the corner of my right eye that the conversation that these two gentlemen were having is starting to get a little more heated with every shot of Patron they took (you got to keep your head on a swivel in a place like this). So during what I believe was the 11th round of the fight, all of the sudden the Akon song

"Smack That" which was playing abruptly stops, and one of the men says really loudly . . .

Thuggish black man 1
(Aggressively)
Just cuz he sucked my dick don't make me no faggot!

One guy in the back of the bar
(Yells)
What the Fuck!

Another guy in the back of the bar
(Yells)
Oh yes it does!

I didn't look at him cuz I didn't wanna be confused with wanting to suck his dick!!!

"Rock star lifestyle might don't make it. Living life high everyday click wasted" are some catchy lyrics to recite, but I don't think Gucci Mane is the guy you want to pattern your drinking habits after.

The Life Lesson, by James LeGrand

Alcohol may be legal, but too much can lead to a bad situation.

How many stories have you heard that started out with, "So I was out drinking when . . . .". Fortunes have been lost, friendships have been ended, love relationships have been destroyed, and negative reputations have been formed because of it. We should all be a little more careful with our alcohol consumption or just avoid it altogether.

As this story shows, alcohol can be a truth serum. Unfortunately, while under the influence, it can be difficult to just stop talking about things and people you shouldn't be talking about at that time. You may say or do something that you can't take back later.

Alcohol leads to fights over the silliest things. I've seen two men fight over their favorite sports team. I've seen women fight comments one made to the other over a dress, hair style or choice of make up. I've seen couples fight over events that happened years ago in the past. I've seen the best of friends start fights with "so you think you are better than me?"

While my brother Abdul abstains from alcohol completely, I have a two-drink rule. Even if I'm not driving, if I'm at an event or around a lot of people, I only have two-drinks, and I space them out pretty well over the evening. I do this so that I can have fun, enjoy the company, but also so I can keep my wits about me and remain in control of my mouth. As a Sifu in Shaolin Kungfu, I cannot afford to lose control. Also, as a husband, father, and many of the roles I've taken on professionally,

I cannot lose it, as there is a lot I could lose by doing so.

Don't allow alcohol to be the spark that makes you lose something or someone that you didn't want to lose. When you decide that you will drink to get wasted, you just may be wasting an important part of your life by doing so.

Take 16: We Treat You Right

The Story, by Abdul Majid

Here's a short story I had to share with you because even as I write this, I can't stop laughing.

After a long day of doing nothing I decided to treat myself with something tasty, and what could be tastier treat on a warm summer's night then an ice-cold Oreo Cookie Blizzard form Dairy Queen. So I go to the local Dairy Queen on South Avenue in Plainfield, New Jersey to purchase my diabetes in a cup. After paying for it, I go to my truck that was parked in the DQ's parking lot to eat this sugary delight. As I sit in the truck shoveling spoonfuls of ice creamy goodness him my face I hear a man begging to this woman on the phone in the car directly next to me. Me being the nosey fucker that I am, I start to listen intently to his conversation.

This man had to be somewhere in his late 40's, balding with a beard and was sitting in a late model (I think it was dark blue or black) Buick with the windows down. As he's going back and forth on the phone with this woman on the other end of his phone, she says something to him loud enough for me to hear from his phone receiver, but too nondescript for me to make out what the hell she was trying to say . . . when all the sudden he responds to her . . .

Cyrano de Bererac
(Sincerely)
Baby I love you so much I had to fuck your sister . . . just to make sure this shit was real.

I swear to God you can't make this shit up!!!!

"The greatest way to live with honor in this world is to is to be what we pretend to be."—Socrates

The Life Lesson, by James LeGrand

Is the person you are with of good moral character?

Yes, I know it has become corny to talk about values, morality and ethics. However, it's the seeking of a high moral character that will ensure you don't have to hear conversations like this on the other end of your telephone!

Character IS important. Men and women without good character will take you on an increasingly more turbulent roller coaster ride in your relationship and dealings with them. They will not always be honest. They will not always do the right thing. They will not always say no when they no they should. Also, they will not always consider the consequences of their actions.

One of the easiest ways to limit or eliminate drama in your life is to exclude anyone (and I do mean anyone) from your life that does not have good character, high moral fiber, and a strong values system. They can be just as fun, but without all of the lies, betrayal and drama.

Take 17: Jersey Drive

The Story, by Abdul Majid

About a month back while sitting in rush hour traffic on Route 22 in Union, NJ I received a phone call from a friend who was returning a call I made to her earlier. Not thinking much of it, I begin to converse with her when all the sudden a police car pulls up behind me and starts to blare its siren. After the normal license and registration check the officer asks me, "Do I know why I pulled you over?" I said "No." After a quick back and forth he gives me a $140 ticket for talking on the cell phone (while I was sitting in fucking traffic). That got me thinking about time when I got my license and some of the rules to the road my father bestowed onto me.

I got my drivers license way back in 1994 when it was a much simpler time. My family couldn't afford to buy me a car and they sure as shit weren't going to let me drive theirs, so all I pretty much had was a driver's license and not much else. To be honest with you I really didn't care because at the time I lived up the street from the train station and I spent most of my time in Brooklyn and Manhattan (like I do now). Driving wasn't as big a deal to me as it was to other suburban kids. Around the same time I received my license, a friend of mine named Eldrick Tont (not real name) also got his license, but unlike me his family had the dough to instantly get him a car.

To give you a little back story, Eldrick and I we first met at Franklin Elementary School in Rahway, NJ in the second grade. We became friends because we both lived in the "Plaza" apartment buildings. We played outside together, rode the same bus to school and ate lunch at the same time, but we really weren't the best of friends. Now as I mentioned in previous stories, I moved around a lot so after I moved from Rahway we didn't keep in touch much until we became familiar again after I moved to Scotch Plains, NJ where he was living.

Unlike many of the other black students going to a predominately white school (80% at the time) Eldrick wasn't the most pro-black person. Whereas many of the other black students in the school were influenced by the hip hop culture that dominated the landscape at the time, (forcing them to wear baggy jeans, African medallions and colorful shirts), Eldrick wasn't moved by that at all.

He was the type of person who if you would ask him if he was black he would go into this long, drawn out, Tiger Woods style dissertation about how he's a cablinasian because his family was one of the original settlers and great, great, great, great, grandfather was Christopher Columbus's butler who was part Cherokee Indian and blah blah, blah. Actually as I think about it I suppose that one of the reason we were friends is because he knew what my mother's ethnicity was and in his mind I guess I past the paper bag test (look it up) and I was a socially acceptable shade of black.

Anyways, he calls me up all excited about getting his license and asks me if I wanted to cruise around Scotch Plains for a while in his new car and look for girls (cuz that's what you do when you live in the suburbs . . . watch any John Hughes movie and you can see that for yourself). After asking my father (yes I still had to ask permission to leave the house because one time I didn't ask and just left and he made me sleep in the car cuz he said "I was tryna' to act grown" . . . but that's another story) and getting permission I called him back and agreed to go on our "Weird Science 2" man expedition.

Now if you ask any black person, they will tell you that the driving laws differ for black people (but especially black men) then they do for whites. My father being the responsible black man and parent thought it would me irresponsible if he didn't give us the rules of the road from the black man's handbook. He explained to us that something as innocent as two black teenage boys going out for a drive after getting their license to a white cop looks like two gang bangers in a stolen car with shotguns, hand grenades and a kilo of cocaine in the trunk looking for a white woman to rape and bludgeon to death before pillaging the community they're driving through in search of a crack pipe to smoke the aforementioned kilo of cocaine in the trunk (or something like that).

He gave us some sound advice like to not make any sudden moves, keep your hands on the steering wheel or in plain sight so they can see them, always make eye contact and to never act fidgety. In the mist of his speech, Eldrick decides to tell him about his family lineage and his lack of bellicose. So my father looks at him with a straight face and says.

My Father
If you get pulled over by the police and they say "Nigga get out of the car" then that means you to . . . . welcome to America nigga.

The best part was the look on his face after my father said that shit. Fucking priceless . . . . that nigga was tight the whole drive.

Race matters and a post-racial America is a façade. Being politically correct is not the same as respecting other people's culture. So if we want better for our society, we have to do better as a society.

The Life Lesson, by James LeGrand

In the face of injustice, we can react or we can respond.

Unfortunately, profiling is still a reality for many in America and around the world. Whether it be the police following you while driving, a store clerk following you around a store, or being selected for a "random screening" every time you fly, profiling is still very much a part of the American culture. Our reaction or response to this injustice can escalate or de-escalate an already bad situation, however.

Reaction (re-act) is when we automatically express ourselves the way we always have whenever we feel victimized, isolated, targeted or singled out. Sometime that reaction is to be calm or it's a reaction based in being passive. For others, the reaction is a rage filled tirade that escalates the situation to a whole new level. It's when we automatically react with anger that we can often make the situation far worse than if we just remained quiet and compliant to get through it. Also, by reacting in this way, we give our follower justification that they had a legitimate reason for following us.

Response is when we consider our actions and expressions before doing anything more to ensure we are de-escalating and disarming the situation. In response, we can prove that the person following or questioning us knows they had nothing to worry about. By doing this, we can change that individuals view of the world one person at a time.

Some of my Caucasian friends think I should react with a lot of anger and make a scene, because that's what works for them when they find themselves in this situation. However, they feel to realize that the unwritten rules are very different in how that situation is handled. They may receive an apology, where I may be thrown out of a store or restaurant.

America remains the best country on the planet to live in as far as I'm currently concerned. However, we have issues like this that continue to persist long after the Civil Right's Movement. Until more changes can occur, its on us to decide how these interactions go.

Take 18: Cleveland Steamer

The Story, by Abdul Majid

I was on my way to Brooklyn driving and listening to the old school at noon on Hot 97, when all the sudden Mister Cee starts cutting up the song that was playing and then fades into a Biggie Smalls record called "Nasty Boy". As I'm rapping the lyrics to the song I begin to laugh hysterically because I started to think back to this precarious situation that I got myself into because of this exact song.

When I was 23 years old, I took a job at a television station in New York called "The Metro Channel". I was one of three audio technicians working for the channel doing field audio and after a late shoot one day, I decided to take a walk through Manhattan. As I'm walking around I see a film crew setting up to shoot a scene, and me being the opportunist that I am I go over check out the set and hopefully get a card from someone so I can give them my resume.

While I'm observing the goings on next to a group of onlookers I see a guy I know working on the film and I call him over. He comes over and after a brief back and forth he invites me onto the set and gives me a mini tour. As we go pass the craft services area, he gets a call on his walkie talkie that one of the actresses is needed on set and he has to get her from the makeup trailer. So I follow him to the makeup trailer and wait for him outside (I was pretending to wait so that I could say bye but I was actually waiting to see who the actress was).

He walks out with "Nasty Girl" (not real name and don't ask who she is cuz I'm not gonna tell anyway). Now Nasty Girl was fine as shit and as he escorts her to the set I tell him I'm about to leave (frontin' hard than a motherfucka). He says to hold on second because he wanted to introduce me to Nasty Girl. He introduces me to her and after a few exchanges (and me name dropping a couple of people that she was friendly with) we started a dialogue. In the mist of our conversation the first A.D. comes over and tells her that they're ready for her on set. As she starts to walk away, she turns around and tells me not to go anywhere because she'll be right back (yup . . . I'm so in).

At this point in the story I'd like to pause for a brief public service announcement. To all the men that might be reading this story, here's a bit of advice on how to pick up a pretty woman. Being around pretty women as much as I am (for occupational as well as scumbag reasons) I find that there are only 2 firm rules you have to obey in order to bag fine ass broad. Rule #1: Never comment on how pretty she is when you first meet her because she hears it all the time. Woman like that are all about the intellect because in my opinion, that aspect of their personality is usually overlooked because of their beauty. They are more apt to engage in a conversation with someone with some depth. So ask as many intelligent questions as you can and don't just be a "yes man". Challenge her on some of her views, but don't be too critical. Rule #2: Be funny! Humor can get you so far it's not even funny. To them funny equals smart which equals sexy, and they like sexy so if you're funny through the transitive properties of syllogism you just became sexy and that much closer to seeing her naked.

Now back to our regularly scheduled story that is already in progress. Fast forward a month and a half later and I'm at her place sitting on the couch and we're joking around. Like two idiots high on weed, we start quoting the interludes to some of our favorite rap album skits. So she starts off with a Wu Tang quote, "I'ma cut your eyelids off and feed you nothing but sleeping pills," to which I respond, "I'ma sew your asshole close and keep feeding you and feeding you." Then she responds with a Biggie Smalls skit "I'ma tell you why I'm mad, I'ma tell you why I'm mad. These niggas is making $500,000 dollar videos, they driving around in hot cars, they got bitches, they got all that shit and I'm still living with my moms . . . that's my word. I'm making records and I ain't make no money yet . . . this my 4th album yo, my 4th album and I ain't made a dime." To which I respond, "I meets this one bitch right, so I comes up to the spot or whatever and the bitch told me she wanted me to shit on her. I'm like shit on you how? I'll shit on you after I hit, I won't call you no more . . . shit on you like that. She said no, she wanted me to cock over and shit on her stomach. I'm like what am I suppose to do after I shit? I'm suppose to hit that? . . . . Boom so after I shits on the bitch".

Now as I'm laughing my ass off, she looks at me with a straight face and asks me if I've ever shitted (the technical term is Coprophilia or Scat) on anyone? Thinking that she was joking I say "I'm gonna shit on you now. Hit them draws and get Swayze" (to all the white people reading this story that means Ghost like the movie Patrick Swayze starred in). So she goes, "No seriously have you ever done it?" to which I respond "Hell no!!!"

Then she asks "Have you ever thought about it?" I respond again "Hell no!!!" She then says "Would you ever do it?" As I give her the "What the fuck?" look, she quickly responds with "It's really not as bad as you think". Now I may not know everything about the human psyche but I do know when I'm being set up to do some shit (no pun intended) that I don't want to do. When a motherfucka says, "It's really not as bad as you think," it kinda usually is.

So now I already know the answer to the question I'm about to ask but I need the confirmation.

Me
Have you shitted on or have been shitted on by anyone?

Nasty Girl
Yes to both

Me
And where do they shit on you?

Nasty Girl
Normally my chest.

Me
(Thinking for a second then getting upset)
You mean I've been sucking on some shitty tittie all this time!?!

To answer your questions; No I didn't do it and Yes this is absolutely a true story!!!

Know what you're getting into before you commit, because everything looks great at the beginning.

The Life Lesson, by James LeGrand

It's important early in relationships to know your partner's sexual history and preferences.

Awkward moments (and sometimes angry moments) happen when not enough discussion takes place or more is assumed than it should be. This is often the case when it comes to sexual preferences like homosexuality or heterosexuality, menage a tois, swinging, oral sex, anal sex, etc. You should know what you are getting into before you get into it. Otherwise, you may not like the surprise that resides on the other side of the interaction.

For the things that you are absolutely looking for or that you absolutely will not do, you should find a way to have that discussion early to ensure you and your potential partner are not barking up the wrong tree. Once you know you are dealing with someone that is within your boundaries, game on! If they are not, then you may not want to play this game with them any longer.

Avoid assumptions. Have the uncomfortable conversation. Get on the same page, and then consenting adults will do what consenting adults choose to do.

Take 19: It Ain't Trickin If You Got It

The Story, by Abdul Majid

One day in November of 2010 while I was checking the mail I notice that I received a coupon booklet from KFC. Now this may seem silly to you but this kind gesture from a corporation pleased me to no end. I'm not sure if you're fully aware of the affects that reduced price fried chicken has on a black man but the aroma alone can excite him to ecstasy and just like cotton "it's the fabric of our lives".

On a Tuesday of that same week I decided for lunch I was going to treat myself to the Colonel's 11 herbs and spices, so I go to the KFC on South Ave in Plainfield, NJ. I walk into the restaurant proudly holding my coupon for a 3-piece meal. As I enter the building I see these four mongrels disguised as woman (1 Spanish, 3 black, 1 of which I am contending is a transsexual) staring at the menu board. They haven't decided what they wanted to order yet, so they let me cut in front of them so I can order my meal.

Now several weeks prior to receiving my coupon booklet I met and began talking to this woman who for the sake of the story we'll call "V for Vendetta". I met Vendetta through a very close friend of mine named "Dinky" who is more like a sister than a friend to me. She came to New York to celebrate her birthday and after meeting her for the first time I was instantly attracted to her. The thing I was most attracted to (besides her ass, titties and bone structure) was her sense of humor. She had one of the sharpest wits I've ever encountered in a female. Not only was she quick witted she had incredible comedic timing and was secure enough with herself that she could make fun of herself as well.

To someone like me who prides himself on his sense of humor and quick wit to find a female with a similar douche baggy sense of humor is rare. We'd spend hours upon hours telling stories, talking shit and making fun of people (but mostly making fun of people). Well like the bible says "as iron sharpens iron, man sharpens man" (Proverbs 27:17). Because of my late night sparring session with Vendetta, my jibber jabber was on full tilt and I could go hard body karate with anyone who talked slick.

Now back at the KFC, I order my food, hand the cashier my coupon, paid, then waited for my meal. As I'm waiting for my order to arrive the "Pack leader" of the mongrels (as Cesar Millan would call them) decides to spark up a flirty conversation with me. She asks me about my coupon then through some form a canine reasoning (of which

I still don't understand) she suggests I pay for her and her friend's meals. I reply, "Why would I do that". She says that it would be the nice thing to do, and I say sarcastically laughing "So is charity but I haven't done that in a while either". She laughs then says to me . . .

Pack Leader
How about you think of it as our first date?

Me
(Sarcastically)
Paying for you guy's meal would be our first date? Sounds more like trickin' to me.

Pack Leader
Well you known they say trickin' is the new dating?

Me
(Sarcastically)
Well if that's the case then your mouth is the new birth control!

I was unaware that birth control was such a sensitive topic for mongrels because the room got quiet for like 5 to 7 seconds. Then those bitches threw some disrespect my way . . . the kind that legends are made of. I was called a "Sucka ass nigga", told to "Get the fuck up out of here with that dumb shit" and told to "Suck my dick" from the tranny!!!!

Civics are not just a car by Honda. It's a social science that we have to practice more often in a civilized society. Start off by treating others as you would want to be treated.

The Life Lesson, by James LeGrand

We've seem to have lost a basic respect for one another as human beings.

I once watched a man having a hear attack fully surrounded by a crowd of people watching him have the heart attack before I jumped in, comforted him and commanded someone to call 9-1-1. What's happened where we've become so disconnected from people that we would rather take a picture of such an event rather than to assist?

We each need to get back to seeing people as people, and not as opportunities, entertainment, a benefit or a detriment, or as a payday. In this story, the leader of this group felt very comfortable asking a total stranger to pay for her meal, and the meals of her friends with the promise of some form of connection afterwards. While she has the right to ask or say whatever she wants, she should also maintain a reasonable understanding of the most likely responses to her request.

Times are hard today, and from what I can tell, they will be harder in the future. We need to go back to the times of people respecting people for no other reason than they are people. We have to learn the appropriateness of circumstance, timing and relationship. We have to stop thinking "I can post a pic to Youtube" first and think, "how can I help" first.

Take 20: Wu Tang Is For The Children

The Story, by Abdul Majid

Lately I've been thinking about how fast the time has gone by and how I still feel like the same asshole I was in high school. It's like some nigga version of arrested development, but it includes questionable nigga shit that can be prosecuted as crimes in several states. Well recently for some strange reason, my aunt thought that it would be a good idea for me to talk to her son because he's been messing up in school. As a single parent, she felt like he needed some male advice on life (so enter The Abdul).

As she's asking me to talk to her son, I'm looking at her like "Nigga do you know me?" At that very moment I start having flashbacks of the time I got caught by my father smoking weed, and the time I stole my fathers car and took it for a joy ride with my boy Tieshone (Yup, that sound you hear is me throwing you under the bus nigga . . . beep beep!!!). I'm sitting there deciding on whether or not I should call DYFS because her parenting skills are in question at the moment. Without thinking this thing through (which should give you a good idea about how this thing ends) I agree to her request and away we go.

I go to his room to have a heart to heart with him like in that episode of the "Cosby Show" were Heathcliff had to talk to Theo about his grades and did the whole analogy about life using the Monopoly money. Since that episode ended well, I decided to do the same thing (but without the Monopoly money). Now I swear to you, I went in there with the best of intentions. I tried my best to present myself as this wise avuncular figure who understood the trials and tribulations of a black man in this cold, racist, unforgiving world he had to contend with. I heard his reasons (more like excuses) and tried to give a counter point and explain to him how he should approach his life and the people in it.

In the middle of my dissertation while sitting at his desk, I accidentally hit his computer mouse and a screen full of porn pops up. My initial reaction was something like "Come on man, what the fuck . . . what if your mother would have came in here and saw this shit on your computer. Then what? You need to start showing her some more respect," give or take a few extra profanities. But upon further review, I noticed that he was watching all Euro porn (meaning porn with all white people in it, not European pornography) and I break character and turn into some ranting porn racist.

I start to go in on him like "What you couldn't find no black people on this motherfucka?" and "Oh what, the white bitches is what's really good? Is that what you're telling me?" I even start to use pseudo black history like "I know Fredrick Douglas didn't worked his ass off just so you could hate your race and be brainwashed by the man's porn" (yes I called it "the man's porn," like I was in The Fruit of Islam and my nationalistic pride was on the line or something).

He starts to relent like "No, no, it's not even like that" and "I couldn't find any good sights" and I'm just getting more frustrated with every excuse. A quick sidebar, but is it just me or at the point when someone admits that they're a nasty motherfucka your current surroundings starts to turn into some Salvador Dali surrealist painting. Depending on the angle at which you look at shit, everything starts to look a little questionable and a bit nasty. I was cool at first and didn't suspect anything. But when he confessed to being a jack off monster I started to question shit like why was the lotion so god damn close (and open) and what the fuck was that crunchy shit I stepped on when I walked into this repugnant, Jackson Pollack cum stained sheets having room.

Anyway . . . . I know in my heart I was wrong for telling him this shit but my brain was so confounded by the fact that he didn't know who Pinky was (and if you're a Black man and don't know who she is you should be ashamed of yourself . . . I said ASHAMED!!! The things she can to do a dick is just . . . . just look it up). I started to show him web sites like Pornotube, Redtube and Youporn and began giving him names of movies and "actresses" to look for. My speech on self-pride and responsibility turned into a comprehensive film studies class on modern pornography and the Strasberg verses Meisner porn acting techniques.

By the end of my disquisition, all the information I had given him had this little nigga's eyes glowing like I just showed him the Arch of the Covenant. So our conversation ends and I get up and walk towards the door when he says . . .

Little Cousin
You think I should tell my mom we had this talk or just keep this between us?

Me
Nigga are you retarded? Why the fuck would you tell your mother? No wonder you're failing school! (Then I slammed the door shut)

If you've ever asked me why I don't have any kids it's because of shit like this!!!

"If you wanna be somebody, if you wanna go somewhere, you better wake up and pay attention"—Whoopi Goldberg from Sister Act 2: Back in the Habit

The Life Lesson, by James LeGrand

Education remains the key doorway to living a happy and fulfilling life doing what you would like to do.

It is very difficult to become a professional or Olympic athlete. Only the rare person finds themselves with the ability and the opportunity to attempt such a life for themselves. For the rest of us, education is a pathway designed for most of us to open the doors we would like to open. Instead of now needing a natural athletic talent or skill, hard work and productive consistency is required, which we can all muster on request.

Unemployment is often lower for college graduates than those that have not attended college. Most management positions require either a lot of experience or a college level degree. It almost doesn't matter what college you attend for most jobs. What matters most is that you attended and graduated college. Before dismissing this out of hand, think about the college graduates in your life. For every Mark Zuckerberg and Bill Gates college drop out success story are thousands of "I wish I took school more seriously" stories.

Regardless of whether you attended college or not, it remains important to continuously educate yourself. There are books and websites on just about everything. Today, you can self teach your way into any new knowledge base through reading, online or face to face courses and video. Today you can even attend classes or coaching sessions via video chat.

Education takes on many forms today. Find a way to continue learning that doesn't put you into unimaginable debt, but that does provide you with the best opportunities to succeed in your chosen profession.

Take 21: When The Chickens Come Home to Roost

The Story, by Abdul Majid

I talk a lot of shit!!! Now I know that statement was no surprise to anyone who knows me, is related to me, has spoken to me or for that matter just watched me sitting there quietly (I even look like I talk a lot of shit). But since the start of the new millennium my shit talking has risen to heights unimaginable. It's like my shit talking has become in sync with the Mayan long count and is trying to talk as much shit as possible before someone turns the lights out on this crazy planet. It's gotten so bad that I involuntarily talk shit to people in my dreams like I'm suffering some neuropsychiatric Tourette disorder.

I've conditioned myself so much that I'm now at the point were it's just some Pavlovian response to any question asked or statement made. I think I've advance far beyond the regular shit talking to an extrasensory type of shit talking. I can astrologically predict future shit talking based on the alignment of the stars and if Saturn is in retrograde (by the way if you're a Sagittarius with Leo rising, it's your ass on Tuesday).

Well about two summers ago during my bodhisattva, I was invited to a cookout by an acquaintance I knew through a friend of a friend. Now normally I would have agreed to go but then just have not shown up but a wise man (or it might have been a homeless man) once said to me "Never pass up free food or money" (damn this economy). So I go to this festive gathering looking only to eat, make a plate to go and be out.

In the mist of my food consumption, this guy who we'll refer to as "The Douche" starts talking shit. At this point my antennas immediately go up and to paraphrase Janet Jackson, "Like a moth to a flame burnt by the fire, my shit talkin's blind can't you see my desire . . . that's the way shit talking goes". I have to admit for the first few minutes or so I stayed quiet sizing up my opponent, listening to his rants, looking for any weak points I could exploit and in my best Conan the Barbarian voice "Crush my enemies, see them driven before you and hear the lamentations of their women".

While listening to The Douche go off on a tangent about how strong his pimp game was, he pulls out his cell phone and starts showing pictures of his harem. As I'm looking at these pictures I'm thinking these have to be the ugliest group of bitches ever collected by one human being for the sole purpose of sexual gratification and gasconading.

Simultaneously, as he's putting his phone away, three jokes come to mind and ding, ding, ding, round one begins.

Like Tiger Woods during a practice round at "The Masters," I start teeing off on these atrocious looking women with an unrelenting barrage of insults and calumniations. I especially honed my attacks in on this one particular woman calling her everything from a hermaphrodite to the Chupacabra. My assault was so hysterically vicious, precisely timed, with a marksman like accuracy that all anyone around me could do was laugh. He tried to retaliate with jokes of his own but I shot him down with jokes about them having a child that looked like an Orca that adapted to land.

This was the quintessential irresistible force paradox but instead of and unstoppable force meeting an immovable object it was a shit talking asshole meeting an obnoxious douche bag . . . and the shit talker wins. In my mind I take a bow to a thunderous ovation, then walk off into the sunset singing Kanye West's "Runaway" (Let's have a toast for the douche bag) with my prepackaged plate of food in hand.

Now fast forward two years later as I'm sitting in an office waiting to be interviewed for a job. Guess who walks in to conduct the interview? Yup, The Douche. He takes a seat at his desk, takes a second to realize it's me, then picks up my resume and smirks. At this point I already know I'm not getting this job, so I start to once over the office for flaws to make fun of when I spot a picture situated on the right corner of his desk next to his phone. As I take a closer look, I notice that this is not just any ole picture, but a family portrait . . . and who's the woman in the picture you ask? Yup, the Chupacabra. Not only did he marry the Chupacabra, but they had a kid together (yes, an actual baby goat). So as he sits there smirking at me, already knowing that I'm not getting hired, I look at the picture, then look at him, then look at the picture, then back at him, pause for a second, smirk, then say . . .

Me
You have a beautiful family.

"Let's have a toast for the asshole!!!"—Kanye West from "Runaway"

What goes around comes around and whether you call it God, Karma or the Universe, "For whatsoever a man sows, that shall he also reap."—Galatians 6:7

The Life Lesson, by James LeGrand

You never know whom you will meet as you move up and down the ladder of success, and people do not forget.

I knew a manager who almost literally stepped on everyone he knew to get to an executive level position. The people that worked for him hated him, as he took direct credit for their work, and he never showed appreciation for those that worked hard for him. Two years after his promotion, he was fired for lack of results, and he staff cheered and celebrated his demise. However, they didn't stop there. They alerted their friends at companies he might apply to about him. The result? He found himself out of work for 3 years.

It's important to treat people well in your career, not just out of the fear of blowing an opportunity, but out of the basic respect for yourself to do the job you are paid to do well, and to provide more and more service to those around you. The manager that shares the success is respected. The person who takes responsibility for the results they achieve or do not achieve is trusted with more responsibility. The co-worker that acknowledges the good work of another co-worker earns the respect of all co-workers.

Being a jerk can get you to the top temporarily, but it is the attributes of respect, honor, trust, and loyalty to your employees that will keep you there while keeping your staff happy.

As you move up the ladder of success, bring someone with you, and ask them to bring someone with them. In this way, you are "paying forward" opportunities for others to succeed as well!

Take 22: What Would I Do Without Tittie

The Story, by Abdul Majid

Along the course of my life I've come across many individuals with very interesting pseudonyms, hypocorisms and sobriquets but the 1 that sticks out the most is a guy by the name of Michael Tyrone. Michael Tyrone is a short, black, bald, portly, yam built motherfucka I use to work with in one of the the plethora of soul draining jobs I've done thus far in my life. Now Michael Tyrone hated the name Michael Tyrone because he felt that it had a bad omen to it. See Michael Tyrone was named after 2 brothers who were his next door neighbors and who both happen to have gone to jail for a murder. So Michael Tyrone wanting to go through life without having to catch a body decides to go by his childhood nickname Tittie (yes like the mammary, boobs, bazoongas or my favorite bresticles).

Now how does a child go about being referred to as "Tittie" you ask? Well in the impoverished southern regions of the United Stated, 1 of the many backward ass shit they do (like voting Republican and against their self interest) is to call a boy who happens to be a momma's boy, a tittie boy. I'm not quite sure how this relates to Michael Tyrone cuz this nigga's from Jersey but if a grown ass man wants to be called Tittie who am I to argue . . . I often go by the moniker "Man Pretty" (which is not only a nickname but an accurate description). So working alongside Tittie I come to find out that amongst several things he is skilled at, he is also a mechanic.

Now prior to me finding this out this bit of information, while driving days before I heard my brakes start to squeak and as you all well know, looking for a hook up is a genetic predisposition for most black people, so I asked him to take a look at my truck. We setup a time for later that week so he could do a FREE diagnostic check on my brakes and we decided to meet up at the South Plainfield mini mall on Oak Tree road next to the Motor Vehicles. If you've never been to South Plainfield, New Jersey it is a predominantly white neighborhood with a few black people sprinkled here and there but none of which would come out in the daytime and especially to a mini mall.

The day comes for Tittie to inspect my car so I get to the mini mall early trying to obtain a good parking spot. I get out of the truck and wait over by 1 of the stories (looking like a gravy stain on a crisp white napkin) when I see from a distance a short, black, Nell Carter built person walking in the opposite direction from me. Not really aware of my surroundings I start yelling for him loud . . . and I mean real loud.

Me
(Yelling)
Yo Tittie . . . Tittie . . . Tittie over here!!!!

Some lady
(With an attitude)
You have some nerve!!!

Me
(Confused)
What

I look over and see that of all things I'm standing next to a table with 2 ladies trying to sign people up for a breast cancer awareness walk. The fucked up part was it wasn't even Tittie but an old Indian woman who was going into Motor Vehicles . . . and these motherfuckas actually had the nerve to call the cops on me and said I was yelling out indecencies.

If by chance you are over the age of 30 and someone wants you to refer to them by some idiotic nickname, I don't give a fuck if it's LL Cool J, you refer to that niggas as Todd!!!! Because the only thing worse than having to yell out some immature, embarrassing, self proclaimed titles is to try to explain why you're doing it to a cop.

"Nicknames stick to people, and the most ridiculous are the most adhesive." ~ Thomas C Haliburton

The Life Lesson, by James LeGrand

At all times, be aware of your surroundings.

Today we live in a world where everyone has a cell phone camera and access to immediately post pictures and videos to the Internet. If you inadvertently do or say the wrong thing at the wrong time, you may become the star in the next viral video.

We also seem to be to be dealing with an increasingly sensitive populous that finds offense in everything. Be careful of what you say and whom you say it around. Also, be careful of what you post to the internet, as jobs and job opportunities have been endangered or even lost due to postings to social media sites.

Lastly, remain aware of your physical surroundings. Crime rates tend to rise as desperate people endeavor to do desperate things. With millions of people losing their jobs, their homes and their hopes, and prices for food and fuel rapidly rising and falling, you'll need to pay a lot more attention to who is around you and if they have negative intentions for you.

Don't be a victim. Stay in tuned with what and who is around you at all times, know the appropriateness of your activities, watch what you choose to put on the internet, and know that the number one deterrent for crime is your awareness.

About The Authors

Abdul Majid

Abdul Majid is an experienced screen writer, talent booker and sound engineer. He has worked for "The Metro Channel" on shows like "Full Frontal Fashion", "Behind the Label", and "Reservations Required. Abdul has also booked celebrity and musical guests for "Studio Y" and "The Daily Beat". In addition, Abdul worked with shows like WE's "Style Me", Oxygen Channel's "Race Matters", A&E's "Biography" and Superbowl XXXIX. Abdul secured a film deal for his script "All In The Game" and has been a ghost writer for several prime time television shows.

James LeGrand

James LeGrand is the author of "Evolve!", an Amazon.com best seller in Religion and Spirituality, and an Expert Author with SelfGrowth. com and Ezine Articles.com. James is also a Vice President in a Fortune 500 company, a Life Strategist and a Sifu in Shaolin Kungfu, which has been known for centuries as a pathway to spiritual enlightenment.

Abdul Majid & James LeGrand
Brothers—1993